New Mexico Ecoregions

- Southwestern Tablelands
- Madrean Archipelago
- Chihuahuan Deserts
- Colorado Plateaus
- Southern Rockies
- High Plains
- Arizona/New Mexico Plateau
- Arizona/New Mexico Mountains

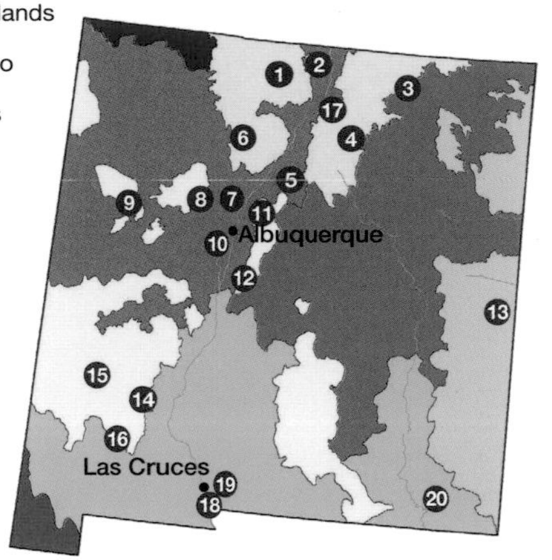

1. Heron Lake State Park
2. Carson National Forest
3. Cimarron Canyon State Park
4. Morphy Lake State Park
5. Santa Fe Canyon Preserve
6. Fenton Lake State Park
7. Corrales Bosque Preserve
8. Petroglyph National Monument
9. Bluewater Lake State Park
10. Rio Grande Botanic Garden
11. Sandia Mountain Wilderness
12. Manzano Mountains State Park
13. Oasis State Park
14. Aldo Leopold Wilderness
15. Gila National Forest
16. City of Rocks State Park
17. Rio Grande Gorge
18. Fabian Garcia Botanical Garden/New Mexico State University
19. Dripping Springs Natural Area
20. Living Desert Zoo & Gardens

Measurements denote the height of plants unless otherwise indicated. Illustrations are not to scale.

N.B. – Many edible wild plants have poisonous mimics. Never eat a wild plant or fruit unless you are absolutely sure it is safe to do so. The publisher makes no representation or warranties with respect to the accuracy, completeness, correctness or usefulness of this information and specifically disclaims any implied warranties of fitness for a particular purpose. The advice, strategies and/or techniques contained herein may not be suitable for all individuals. The publisher shall not be responsible for any physical harm (up to and including death), loss of profit or other commercial damage. The publisher assumes no liability brought or instituted by individuals or organizations arising out of or relating in any way to the application and/or use of the information, advice and strategies contained herein.

Made in the USA

Waterford Press publishes reference guides that introduce readers to nature observation, outdoor recreation and survival skills. Product information is featured on the website: **www.waterfordpress.com**

Text & illustrations © 2009, 2023 Waterford Press Inc. All rights reserved. Photos © Shutterstock. Ecoregion map © The National Atlas of the United States. To order or for information on custom published products please call 800-434-2555 or email orderdesk@waterfordpress.com. For permissions or to share comments email editor@waterfordpress.com.

ISBN 978-1-58355-514-9
$7.95 U.S.
UPC
10 9 8 7 6 5 4 3 2 1
2309326

NEW MEXICO TREES & WILDFLOWERS – A Folding Pocket Guide to Familiar Plants

WATERFORD PRESS

A POCKET NATURALIST® GUIDE

NEW MEXICO TREES & WILDFLOWERS

A Folding Pocket Guide to Familiar Plants

T0123954

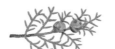

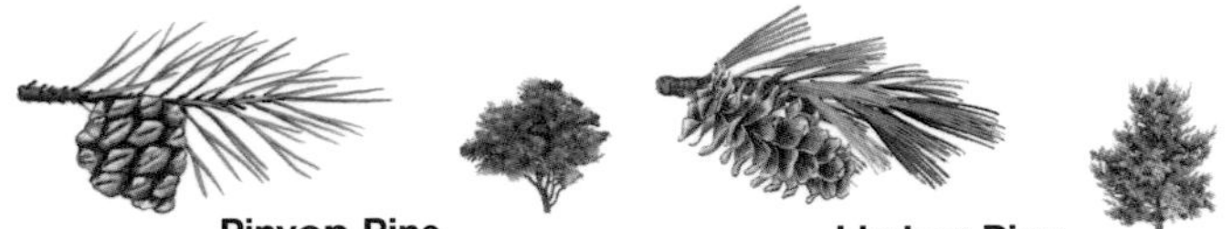

Pinyon Pine
Pinus edulis To 35 ft. (11 m)
Stiff needles grow in bundles of 2 along twigs. Short-stalked, rounded cones produce large seeds.
New Mexico's state tree.

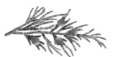

Limber Pine
Pinus flexilis To 50 ft. (15 m)
Needles grow in bundles of 5. Elongate cone has scales thickest at their tips.

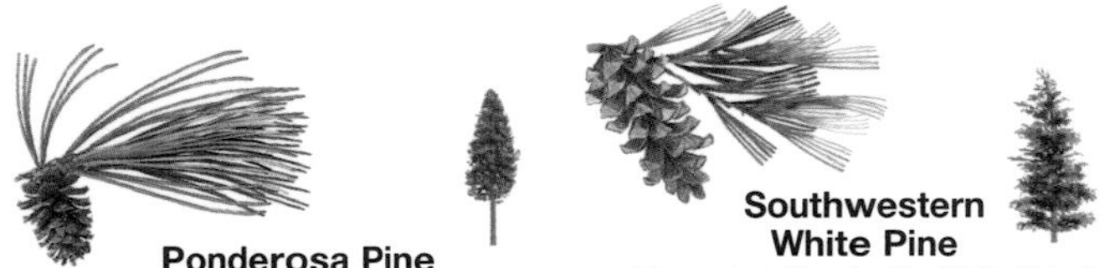

Ponderosa Pine
Pinus ponderosa To 130 ft. (40 m)
Long needles are in bundles of 2 or 3. Cones have scales that have sharp outcurved prickles.

Southwestern White Pine
Pinus strobiformis To 80 ft. (24 m)
Seeds were an important food for Native Americans in the Southwest.

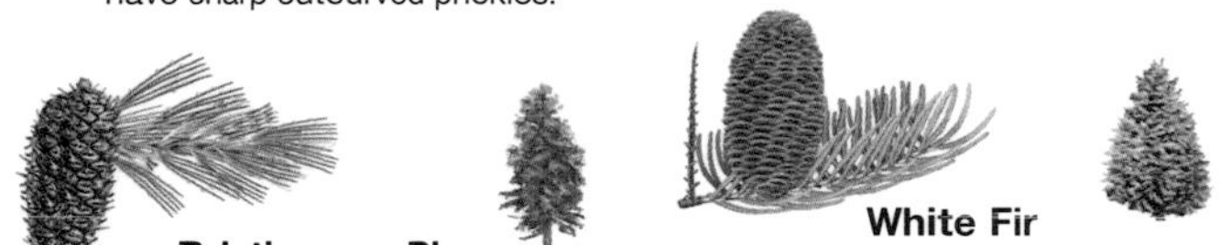

Bristlecone Pine
Pinus aristata To 40 ft. (12 m)
Needles are in bundles of 5 and are densely clustered along branchlets. Cones are purplish and have incurved prickles on their scales.

White Fir
Abies concolor To 160 ft. (49 m)
Cone-shaped tree. Flat, stalkless needles grow singly and curl upwards. Cylindrical cones grow upright from twigs.

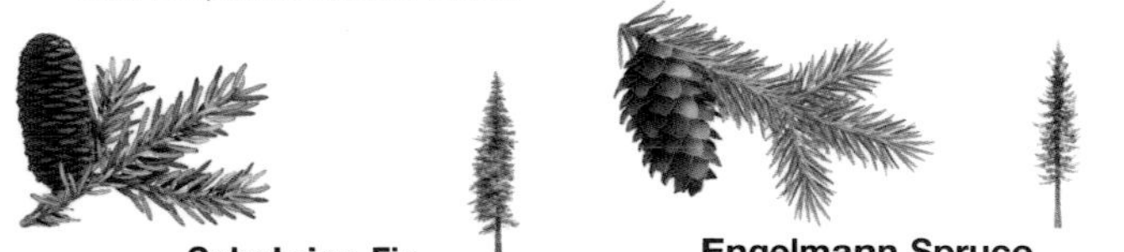

Subalpine Fir
Abies lasiocarpa To 100 ft. (30 m)
Flattened, dark green needles have silvery line on both surfaces. Cylindrical cones grow upright.

Engelmann Spruce
Picea engelmannii To 100 ft. (30 m)
Needles have sharp tips and exude a pungent odor when crushed. Cones often grow in clusters.

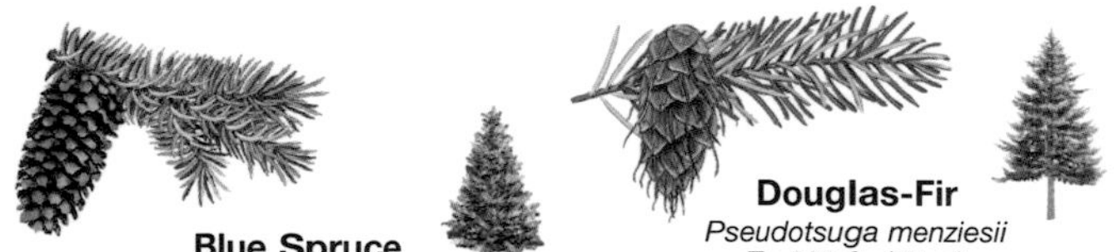

Blue Spruce
Picea pungens To 100 ft. (30 m)
Blue-green needles are up to 1.5 in. (4 cm) long and very prickly. Cones have scales with ragged edges.

Douglas-Fir
Pseudotsuga menziesii
To 200 ft. (61 m)
Flat needles grow in a spiral around branchlets. Cones have 3-pointed bracts protruding between the scales.

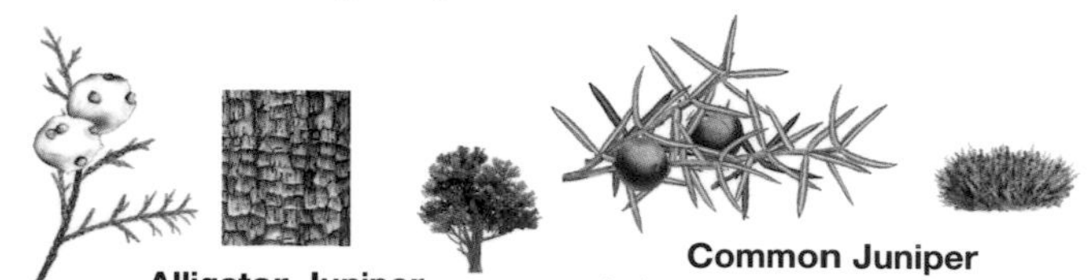

Alligator Juniper
Juniperus deppeana To 50 ft. (15 m)
Opposite leaves grow in four rows. Dark bark is furrowed in thick plates.

Common Juniper
Juniperus communis To 4 ft. (1.2 m)
Needle-like leaves grow in whorls of 3 around twigs. Berry-like, blue-black cones have 1-3 seeds.

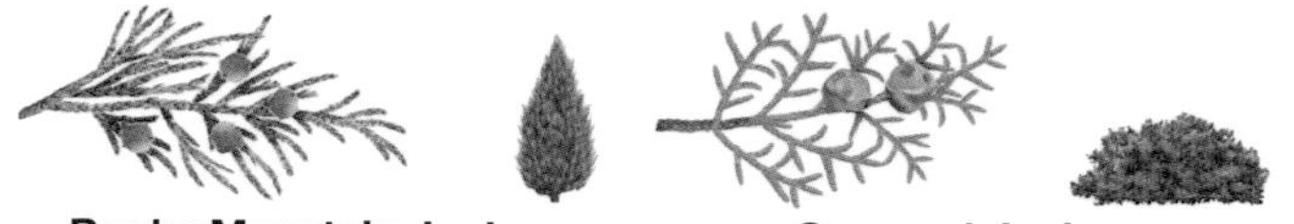

Rocky Mountain Juniper
Juniperus scopulorum To 50 ft. (15 m)
Has bushy crown of ascending branches. Blue, berry-like fruits have a waxy coating.

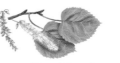

Oneseed Juniper
Juniperus monosperma To 25 ft. (7.6 m)
Shrub or small tree. Bluish, berry-like fruits contain a single seed.

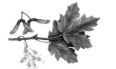

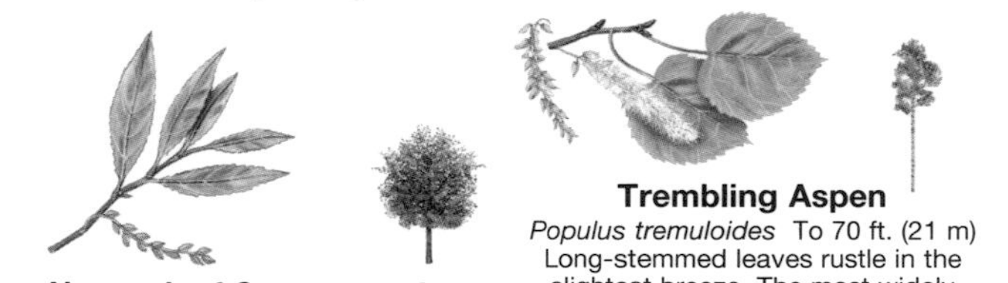

Narrowleaf Cottonwood
Populus angustifolia To 50 ft. (15 m)
Distinguished by its narrow, willow-like leaves.

Trembling Aspen
Populus tremuloides To 70 ft. (21 m)
Long-stemmed leaves rustle in the slightest breeze. The most widely distributed tree in North America.

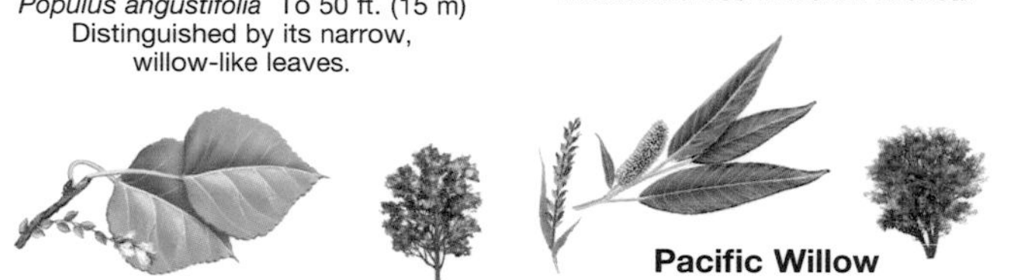

Fremont Cottonwood
Populus fremontii To 80 ft. (24 m)
Heart-shaped leaves have gently-toothed edges and flattened stems. Flowers are succeeded by cottony seeds.

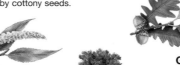

Pacific Willow
Salix lasiandra To 50 ft. (15 m)
Narrow leaves are green above, grayish below.

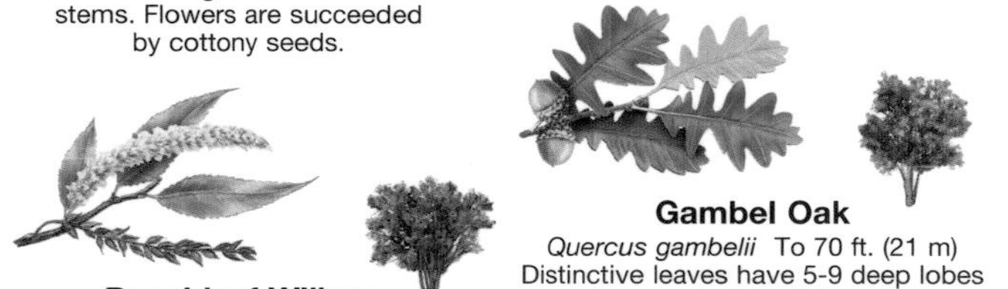

Peachleaf Willow
Salix amygdaloides To 60 ft. (18 m)
Leaves have a yellow-orange midrib.

Gambel Oak
Quercus gambelii To 70 ft. (21 m)
Distinctive leaves have 5-9 deep lobes and are up to 6 in. (15 cm) long. Acorns are broadly oval.

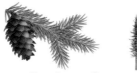

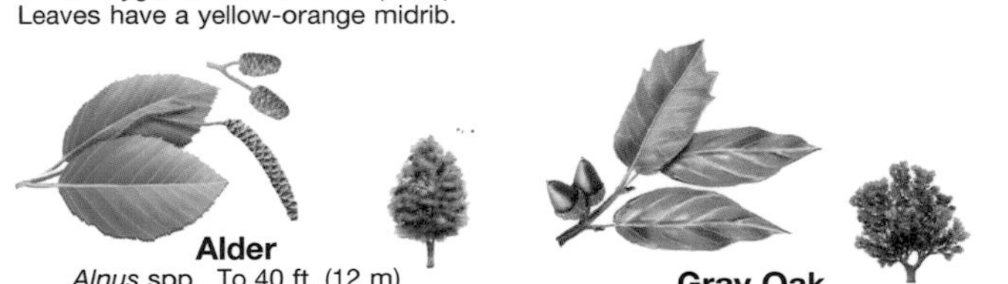

Alder
Alnus spp. To 40 ft. (12 m)
Shrub or tree often forms dense thickets. Flowers bloom in long clusters and are succeeded by distinctive, cone-like woody fruits.

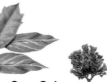

Gray Oak
Quercus grisea To 60 ft. (18 m)
Clump-forming shrub or small tree has grayish foliage. Common on dry, rocky or gravelly soils.

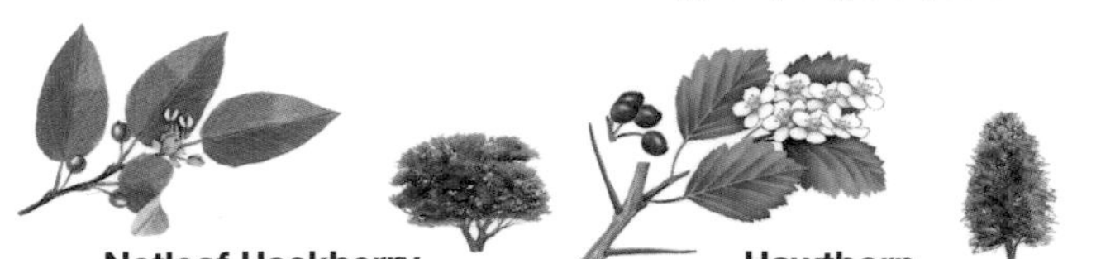

Netleaf Hackberry
Celtis reticulata To 30 ft. (9 m)
Small, short-trunked tree is found near water. Leaves have prominent net-like veins on the lower surface.

Hawthorn
Crataegus spp. To 40 ft. (12 m)
Tree has rounded crown of spiny branches. Apple-like fruits appear in summer.

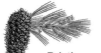

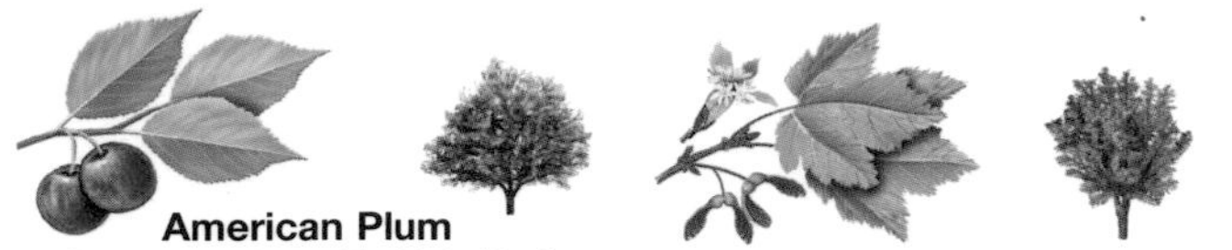

American Plum
Prunus americana To 30 ft. (9 m)
Oval leaves have toothed edges. Bright red fruits have yellow flesh.

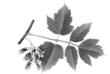

Rocky Mountain Maple
Acer glabrum To 30 ft. (9 m)
Leaves are up to 4.5 in. (11 cm) long and have reddish stalks. Flowers are succeeded by winged seed pairs in late summer.

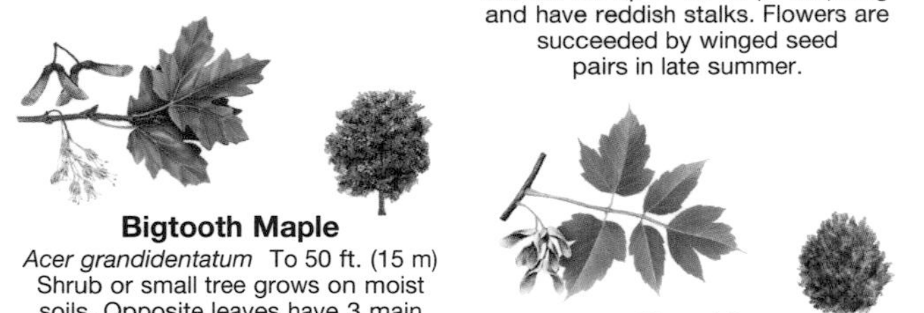

Bigtooth Maple
Acer grandidentatum To 50 ft. (15 m)
Shrub or small tree grows on moist soils. Opposite leaves have 3 main lobes. Fruits have 2-winged.

Boxelder
Acer negundo To 60 ft. (18 m)
Leaves have 3-7 leaflets. Seeds are encased in paired papery keys.

Western Soapberry
Sapindus drummondii To 40 ft. (12 m)
Leaves have 7-19 leaflets. White flowers are succeeded by yellowish berries.

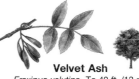

Velvet Ash
Fraxinus velutina To 40 ft. (12 m)
Leaves have 3-5 leaflets. Flowers are succeeded by clusters of single-winged fruits.

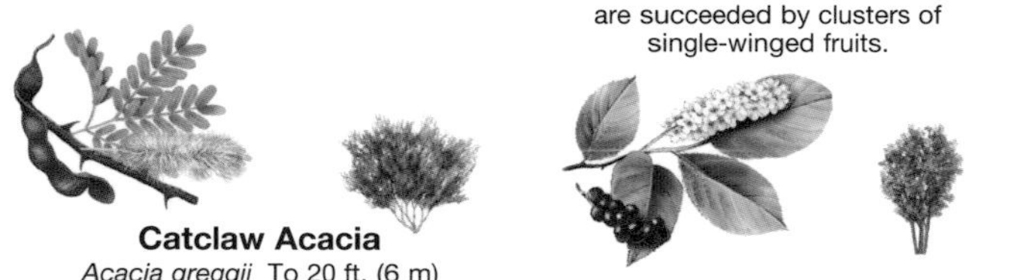

Catclaw Acacia
Acacia greggii To 20 ft. (6 m)
Branchlets are covered with sharp, claw-like spines. Seed pods are twisted.

Common Chokecherry
Prunus virginiana To 20 ft. (6 m)
Cylindrical clusters of spring flowers are succeeded by dark, red-purple berries.

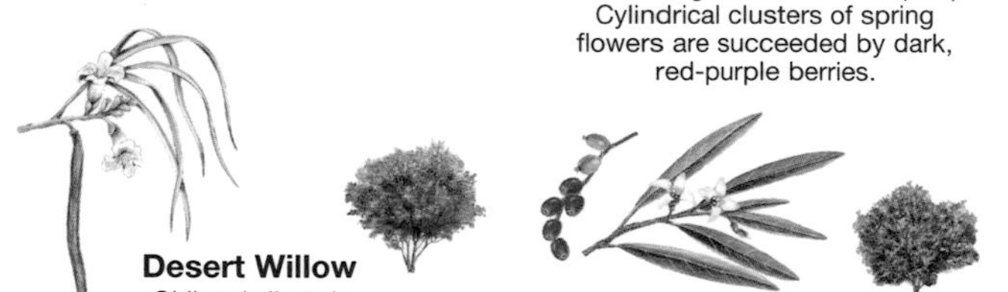

Desert Willow
Chilopsis linearis
To 25 ft. (7.6 m)
Showy flowers bloom May-June and are succeeded by long seed pods.

Russian Olive
Elaeagnus angustifolia To 20 ft. (6 m)
Shrub or small tree has silvery leaves and spiny thorns. A fast-growing plant that was widely planted in shelterbelts.

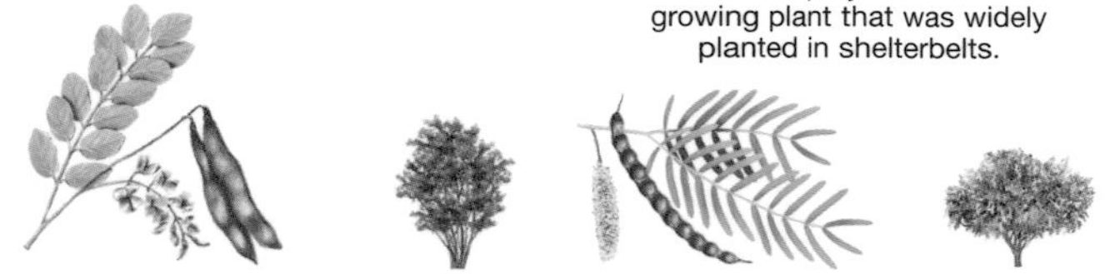

New Mexico Locust
Robinia neomexicana To 25 ft. (7.6 m)
Thicket-forming spiny shrub or tree. Seed pods are covered with bristly hairs.

Honey Mesquite
Prosopis glandulosa To 20 ft. (6 m)
Leaves have 7-20 pairs of leaflets. Seed pods are up to 8 in. (20 cm) long.

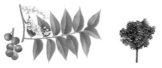

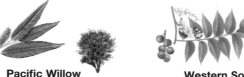

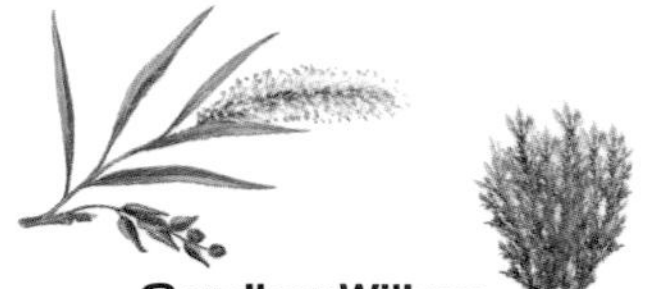

Sandbar Willow
Salix exigua To 10 ft. (3 m)
Shrub forms thickets in wet soils.

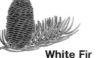

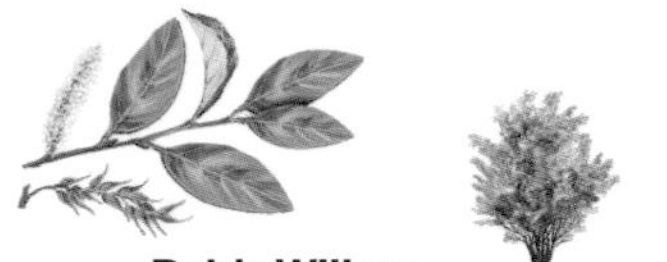

Bebb Willow
Salix bebbiana To 25 ft. (7.6 m)
Oblong leaves are widest at or above the middle and have prominent veins.

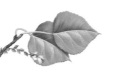

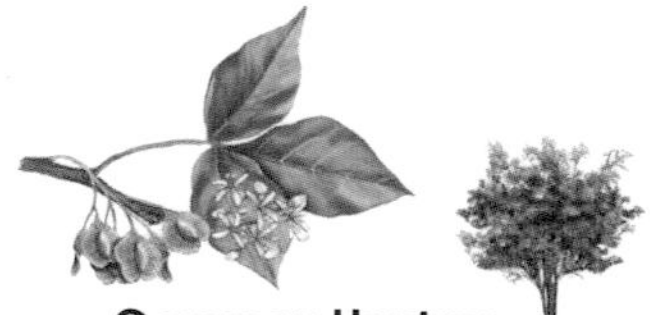

Common Hoptree
Ptelea trifoliata To 20 ft. (6 m)
Shrub or small tree. Leaves have 3 leaflets. Flattened fruits were once used in lieu of hops to brew beer.

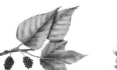

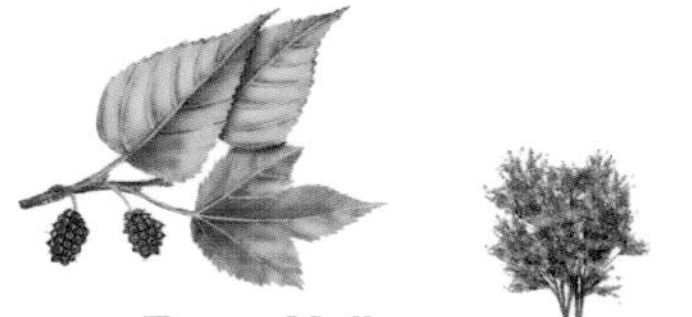

Texas Mulberry
Morus microphylla To 20 ft. (6 m)
Small tree or shrub has variably-shaped leaves and milky sap. Fruit is an edible red berry that blackens with age.

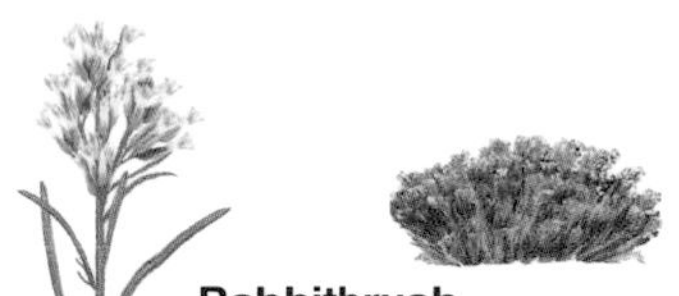

Rabbitbrush
Ericameria nauseosa
To 7 ft. (2.1 m)
Wiry shrub has erect stems that support terminal clusters of small yellow flowers.

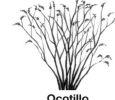

Ocotillo
Fouquieria splendens
To 30 ft. (9 m)
Bright red, tubular flowers bloom at the tips of thorny stems in spring.

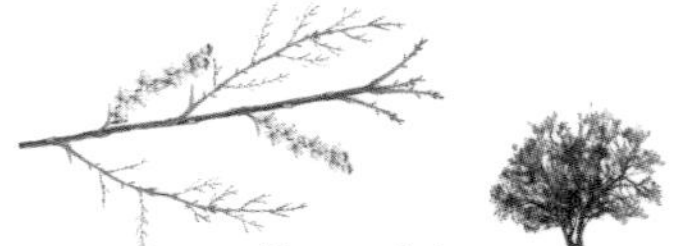

Tamarisk
Tamarix chinensis To 15 ft. (4.5 m)
Wiry twigs are covered in tiny, scale-like leaves. Small pink flowers bloom in summer.

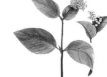

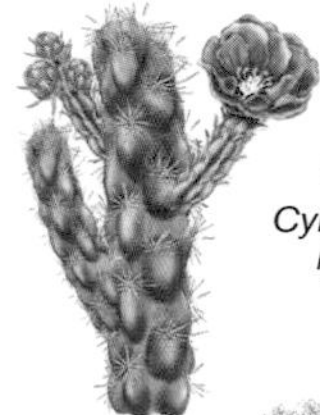

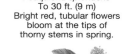

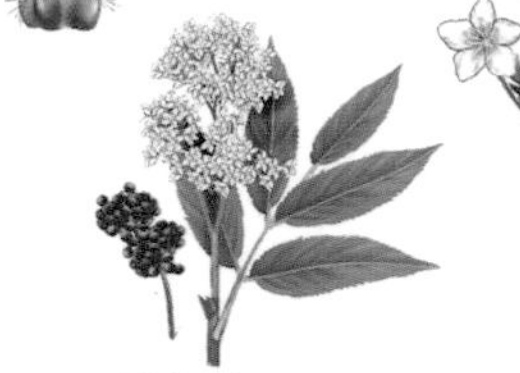

Red-Osier Dogwood
Cornus sericea To 10 ft. (3 m)
Thicket-forming shrub. White flowers are succeeded by waxy white berries. Bark is reddish.

Tree Cholla
Cylindropuntia imbricata
To 15 ft. (4.5 m)

Elderberry
Sambucus spp.
To 15 ft. (4.5 m)
Leaves have 5-7 leaflets and are sharply toothed.

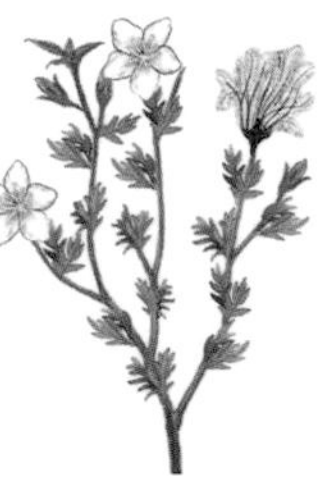

Apache Plume
Fallugia paradoxa
To 7 ft. (2.1 m)

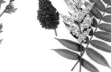

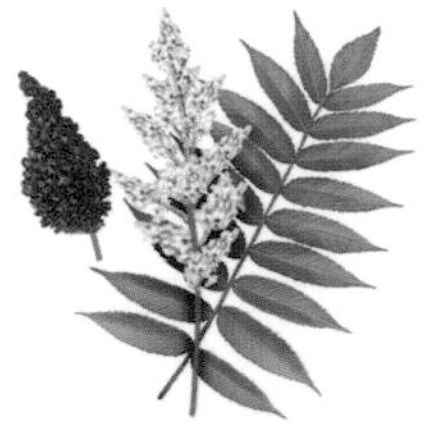

Smooth Sumac
Rhus glabra To 20 ft. (6 m)
Clusters of white flowers are succeeded by "hairy" red fruits. Bark is gray and smooth.

Yarrow
Achillea millefolium
To 3 ft. (90 cm)
Leaves are fern-like.
Each tiny flower
has 4–6 rays.

Rose Heath
Chaetopappa ericoides
To 15 in. (38 cm)

White Locoweed
Oxytropis sericea
To 16 in. (40 cm)

White Milkwort
Polygala alba
To 14 in. (35 cm)

Mariposa Lily
Calochortus spp.
To 20 in. (50 cm)

Poison Milkweed
Asclepias subverticillata
To 4 ft. (1.2 m)

Water Hemlock
Cicuta maculata
To 7 ft. (2.1 m)
Wetland plant has flat-
topped clusters of white
flowers and 2–3 lobed
leaves. All parts of the
plant are poisonous.

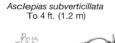

White Prairie Clover
Dalea candida
To 2 ft. (60 cm)

Wild Candytuft
Thlaspi montanum
To 6 in. (15 cm)
Yellow-centered,
white flowers may be
white, yellow, pink, red
or lavender. Grows in
sprawling clusters.

Fleabane
Erigeron spp.
To 3 ft. (90 cm)

Southwestern Thornapple
Datura wrightii
To 5 ft. (1.5 m)
Flowers bloom at
night and are
pollinated by moths.

Phlox
Phlox spp.
To 20 in. (50 cm)
Five-petalled, yellow-
centered flowers can be
white, yellow, pink, red
or lavender. Grows in
sprawling clusters.

White Prairie Aster
Aster falcatus
To 2 ft. (60 cm)

Wild Raspberry
Rubus spp.
To 16 in. (40 cm)
White 5-petalled
flowers are succeeded
by the familiar berry.

Pearly Everlasting
Anaphalis margaritacea
To 3 ft. (90 cm)

Curly Dock
Rumex crispus
To 4 ft. (1.2 m)
Large leaves have curled
or wavy edges. Flowers
are succeeded by small,
heart-shaped winged
seeds. Invasive.

Hooded Ladies' Tresses
Spiranthes romanzoffiana
To 2 ft. (60 cm)

Yucca
Yucca glauca
To 4 ft. (1.2 m)
Large flowers bloom in a
long spike. **New Mexico's
state flower.**

Death Camas
Zigadenus elegans
To 28 in. (70 cm)
Star-shaped,
green-centered
flowers bloom in
a long terminal
cluster. Plant is
highly poisonous.

Blackfoot Daisy
Melampodium leucanthum
To 20 in. (50 cm)

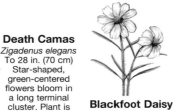

Mountain Dandelion
Agoseris aurantiaca
To 2 ft. (60 cm)

Greeneyes
Berlandiera lyrata
To 4 ft. (1.2 m)
Also called chocolate
flower for its scent.

Desert Marigold
Baileya multiradiata
To 20 in. (50 cm)
Common along
roadsides.

Goldenrod
Solidago spp.
To 5 ft. (1.5 m)
Flowers bloom in
arched clusters.

Western Wallflower
Erysimum capitatum
To 3 ft. (90 cm)

Fringed Puccoon
Lithospermum incisum
To 12 in. (30 cm)

Common Sunflower
Helianthus spp.
To 13 ft. (3.9 m)
Flowers follow the sun
across the sky each day.

Plains Prickly Pear
Opuntia spp.
Pads to 6 in. (15 cm)
Pads grow in clumps up
to 12 ft. (3.6 m) wide.

Yellow Monkeyflower
Mimulus guttatus
To 3 ft. (90 cm)
Flowers are
trumpet-shaped.

Cinquefoil
Potentilla spp.
To 3 ft. (90 cm)
Small, shrubby plant
has bright yellow,
waxy flowers.

Little Golden Zinnia
Zinnia grandiflora
To 9 in. (22 cm)

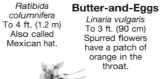

Coneflower
Ratibida columnifera
To 4 ft. (1.2 m)
Also called
Mexican hat.

Butter-and-Eggs
Linaria vulgaris
To 3 ft. (90 cm)
Spurred flowers
have a patch of
orange in the
throat.

Cutleaf Coneflower
Rudbeckia laciniata
To 6 ft. (1.8 m)

Green Pitaya
Echinocereus viridiflorus
To 10 in. (25 cm)

Golden Columbine
Aquilegia chrysantha
To 4 ft. (1.2 m)
Flowers have
prominent spurs.

Buttercup
Ranunculus spp.
To 3 ft. (90 cm)
Flower petals are
waxy to the touch.

Yellow Salsify
Tragopogon dubius
To 3 ft. (90 cm)

Cowpen Daisy
Verbesina encelioides
To 5 ft. (1.5 m)

Nodding Onion
Allium cernuum
To 2 ft. (60 cm)
Pinkish flowers bloom
in a nodding cluster.

Scarlet Gaura
Gaura coccinea
To 2 ft. (60 cm)

Indian Paintbrush
Castilleja spp.
To 3 ft. (90 cm)

Redstem Filaree
Erodium cicutarium
To 20 in. (50 cm)
Invasive.

New Mexico Thistle
Cirsium neomexicanum
To 6 ft. (1.8 m)

Pincushion Cactus
Coryphantha vivipara
To 6 ft. (1.8 m)

Fireweed
Chamerion angustifolium
To 10 ft. (3 m)
Common in open
woodlands and
waste areas.

Milkweed
Asclepias speciosa
To 4 ft. (1.2 m)
Leaves and
stem are sticky.

Clammyweed
Polanisia dodecandra
To 32 in. (80 cm)
Plant is covered with
sticky hairs.

Hedgehog Cactus
Echinocereus triglochidiatus
To 12 ft. (3.6 m)
Cylindrical stems grow
in clusters. Flowers
bloom in spring.

Rocky Mountain Bee Plant
Cleome serrulata
To 5 ft. (1.5 m)
Leaves have 3
narrow leaflets.

Firewheel
Gaillardia pulchella
To 2 ft. (60 cm)

Skyrocket
Ipomopsis aggregata
To 7 ft. (2.1 m)
Flowers resemble
exploded fireworks.

Beardtongue
Penstemon barbatus
To 3 ft. (90 cm)
Lower lip and throat
of flower is "bearded"
with fine hairs.

Wild Rose
Rosa spp.
To 5 ft. (1.5 m)

Wild Geranium
Geranium spp.
To 2 ft. (60 cm)

Violet Wood Sorrel
Oxalis spp.
To 6 in. (15 cm)

Mountain Bluebell
Mertensia ciliata
To 5 ft. (1.5 m)

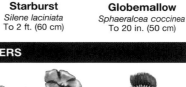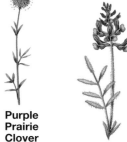

Desert Four O'Clock
Mirabilis multiflora
To 18 in. (45 cm)

Starburst
Silene laciniata
To 2 ft. (60 cm)

Scarlet Globemallow
Sphaeralcea coccinea
To 20 in. (50 cm)

Harebell
Campanula rotundifolia
To 40 in. (1 m)

Common Morning Glory
Ipomoea spp.
Stems to 10 ft.
(3 m) long.
Creeping plant.

Nodding Thistle
Carduus nutans
To 9 ft. (2.7 m)

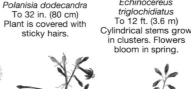

Rocky Mountain Iris
Iris missouriensis
To 20 in. (50 cm)

Spiderwort
Tradescantia spp.
To 3 ft. (90 cm)

Lupine
Lupinus spp.
To 2 ft. (60 cm)
Note star-shaped leaves.

Sticky Aster
Machaeranthera bigelovii
To 3 ft. (90 cm)

Wild Bergamot
Monarda fistulosa
To 4 ft. (1.2 m)

New Mexico Phacelia
Phacelia neomexicana
To 30 in. (80 cm)

Blue Violet
Viola spp.
To 8 in. (20 cm)

American Vetch
Vicia americana
Stems to 7 ft. (2.1 m) long.
Climbing or sprawling
plant has tubular, pea-
shaped flowers.

Dotted Gayfeather
Liatris punctata
To 31 in. (78 cm)

Dayflower
Commelina spp.
To 3 ft. (90 cm)
Flowers have two
large blue petals
above a tiny
white one.

Purple Prairie Clover
Dalea purpurea
To 3 ft. (90 cm)

Purple Locoweed
Oxytropis lambertii
To 16 in. (40 cm)

Silverleaf Nightshade
Solanum elaeagnifolium
To 3 ft. (90 cm)

Larkspur
Delphinium spp.
To 6 ft. (1.8 m)
5-part flowers have
prominent spurs.

Bluets
Houstonia spp.
To 6 in. (15 cm)
Yellow-centered flowers
grow in large colonies.